THE BETTY & BARNEY HILL
ALIEN ABDUCTION

By Chris Bowman
Illustration By D. Brady
Color By Gerardo Sandoval

BELLWETHER MEDIA • MINNEAPOLIS, MN

383 2393

STRAY FROM REGULAR READS
WITH BLACK SHEEP BOOKS.
FEEL A RUSH WITH EVERY READ!

Library of Congress Cataloging-in-Publication Data

Names: Bowman, Chris, author.
Title: The Betty & Barney Hill Alien Abduction / by Chris Bowman.
Description: Minneapolis, MN : Bellwether Media, Inc., 2020. | Series: Black Sheep: Paranormal Mysteries | Includes
    bibliographical references and index. | Audience: Grade: 3 to 7. |
Identifiers: LCCN 2019003756 (print) | LCCN 2019005073 (ebook) | 9781618916655 (ebook) |
    ISBN 9781644870938 (hardcover : alk. paper) | ISBN 9781618917317 (pbk. : alk. paper)
Subjects: LCSH: Alien abduction–New Hampshire–Juvenile literature. | Unidentified flying objects–
    Sightings and encounters–New Hampshire–Juvenile literature. | Hill, Betty (Eunice)–Juvenile literature. |
    Hill, Barney, 1922-1969–Juvenile literature.
Classification: LCC BF2050 (ebook) | LCC BF2050 .B725 2020 (print) | DDC 001.942–dc23
LC record available at https://lccn.loc.gov/2019003756

Editor: Christina Leaf   Designer: Andrea Schneider

Printed in the United States of America, North Mankato, MN.

TABLE OF CONTENTS

Red text identifies
historical quotes.

In the 1960s, newspapers printed a wild tale. A couple claimed to have been **abducted** by an alien spacecraft! The world watched as Betty and Barney Hill told their story...

The Portsmouth Herald

Late at night on Sept. 19, 1961, they were driving through the White Mountains of New Hampshire, returning from a Canadian vacation to their home in Portsmouth when they spotted an object in the sky with lights, which at first seemed like an airplane. But when the "airplane" began to rapidly descend in their direction, they quickly continued driving south along Route 3.

Just south of the Indian Head resort, the Hills stopped in the middle of the road and said the silent, cigar-shaped craft hovered above their car. Through binoculars, Barney claimed to see several "strangely not human" figures

Local Couple UFO Experience

September 19, 1961, just before midnight: Betty and Barney Hill drive south down Route 3 in New Hampshire. They are returning home from a vacation in Canada.

Beautiful night.

It sure is.

September 21, 1961:
Betty calls the Pease Air Force Base to report their experience.

Major Paul W. Henderson reports their story in the military's Project Blue Book, which deals with **UFO** sightings.

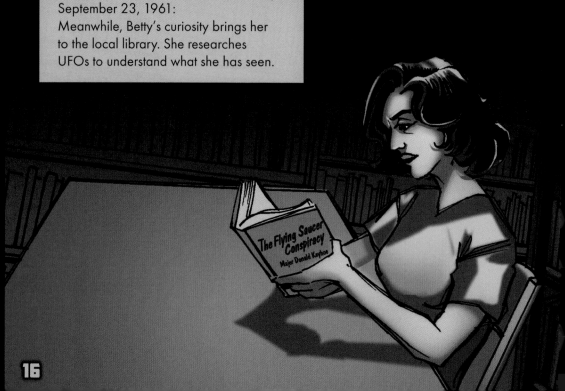

September 23, 1961:
Meanwhile, Betty's curiosity brings her to the local library. She researches UFOs to understand what she has seen.

The Flying Saucer Conspiracy
Major Donald Keyhoe

Soon after, Betty has nightmares. She dreams of being taken to a clearing in the woods and on board an alien spacecraft.

Betty is not the only one with side effects. Barney gets headaches and has trouble sleeping. Their dog, Delsey, becomes sick, too.

The Hills decide to try a new approach.

We need answers about that night.

Maybe we should try **hypnotism**?

Betty and Barney contact a **psychiatrist**. But he recommends waiting on hypnosis in case more memories arise. Then, that fall, Barney has a breakthrough. He recounts his new memory to Betty and her parents.

What happened then?

We came to the roadblock. And then...

December 14, 1963:
With this memory, the Hills decide to be hypnotized. They meet with Dr. Benjamin Simon to plan the treatment.

I'll meet with each of you separately during these appointments.

Following months of planning, Betty and Barney begin the process. Under hypnosis, they remember more details from that night. They both remember medical tests.

Betty remembers communicating with one of the aliens. They show her a book and a star map.

At the end of their tests, Betty and Barney are brought back to the car separately.

Will we remember this?

No.

Since then, people have debated what happened to Betty and Barney. Some experts have matched Betty's description of the star map with the distant star system Zeta Reticuli.

Skeptics have searched for other explanations. Some think the Hills had just seen a spotlight.

Believers and skeptics are still amazed by the Hills' experience. The world will likely never know the truth behind their story.

THEORIES BEHIND THE ABDUCTION

- At first, the Air Force suggests that the Hills may have seen searchlights.

- In Project Blue Book, the Air Force suggests that the bright light the Hills saw was the planet Jupiter.

- Some people believe that the Hills may have seen a weather balloon.

- Other people suggest that the abduction never happened. Betty had nightmares, which people said Barney came to believe he had experienced as well.

- Some skeptics have also suggested that the buzzing noises heard by the Hills were caused by the trunk. They say Barney forgot to latch it before they started driving.

TIMELINE

September 19-20, 1961: Betty and Barney Hill believe they are abducted by aliens while driving home

September 23, 1961: Betty begins investigating UFOs

September 21, 1961: The Hills report their experiences to the nearby Air Force base

Around September 30, 1961: Betty begins having nightmares

Glossary

abducted—taken by force and without permission

binoculars—an instrument used to see objects that are far away

compass—an instrument that uses magnets to determine direction

hypnotism—the act of being put into a sleep-like state in which people will respond easily to suggestions

psychiatrist—a doctor who treats mental, emotional, or behavioral disorders

satellite—an object that orbits Earth

skeptical—having doubts

therapy—treatment to help someone heal; many people use therapy to work through painful memories or experiences.

UFO—an unidentified flying object; UFOs are often thought to be alien spacecraft, although any unknown flying object can be called a UFO.

December 14, 1963: The Hills decide to be hypnotized

October 25, 1965: The Hills learn that their story is in the newspapers

To Learn More

AT THE LIBRARY

Borgert-Spaniol, Megan. *UFOs: Are Alien Aircraft Overhead?* Minneapolis, Minn.: Abdo Pub., 2019.

Hoena, Blake. *The Roswell UFO Incident.* Minneapolis, Minn.: Bellwether Media, 2020.

Owings, Lisa. *Alien Abductions.* Minneapolis, Minn.: Bellwether Media, 2019.

ON THE WEB

FACTSURFER

Factsurfer.com gives you a safe, fun way to find more information.

1. Go to www.factsurfer.com
2. Enter "Betty and Barney Hill" into the search box and click 🔍.
3. Select your book cover to see a list of related web sites.

Index

OYSTER BAY-E NORWICH PUB LIBY
89 EAST MAIN ST
OYSTER BAY, NY 11771
(516) 922-1212